- To my boys -

I love you with all my heart.

Your existence makes me a better person everyday.

Thank you for all that you do and for all that you are!

With unconditional love,

- Momma -

Flyer Junior was excited. It was his first day back to school from winter break.

On days with such beautiful weather all the Flyers spend the day outside learning at Sebastian Flight Academy.

When Junior arrived at school, all the other flyers said, "Hi, Junior." Junior immediately smiled. It felt nice to have so many friends.

The teacher told Junior, "We have a new student. He's over in the housekeeping section."

After listening to his teacher, about the new student, Junior started playing with his flyer friends Sophia, Anthony, Cooper, and Noah.

While playing with his friends, Junior kept looking over at the new student. He didn't feel right on the inside of his tummy and he could tell the new student was scared and lonely.

Junior decided to roll over to the new student. Junior felt nervous. He didn't know what to say when he got there.

Just then, Junior remembered Momma Flyer telling him when you meet someone new and you don't know what to say, just start with "Hi" and tell them your name.

Junior did just that. He rolled over and said, "Hi, I am Flyer Junior." The new student smiled and replied, "Hi, I'm Choppie."

Junior had never seen anyone who looked like Choppie before. His propellers were on top of his head and not on his nose like the rest of his friends.

Junior looked back and saw his friends staring at him. They were wondering what he was doing. Junior got nervous. He thought, "What if my friends don't want to be my friends anymore because I am talking to Choppie?"

At that moment, Junior remembered something else Momma Flyer had told him. "We don't judge our friends by how they look." Junior always wanted to make his Momma proud, but he didn't want his friends to stop playing with him either.

That's when Junior knew what the right thing to do was. He heard his Momma saying in his head, "Ask Choppie to come play with you and your other friends."

Choppie was so excited to be asked to play. Junior and Choppie rolled over to the other flyers. Junior introduced Choppie to all the flyers and said, "Look what Choppie's propellers do!" All the flyers looked in amazement as Choppie twirled his propellers above his head.

All the flyers smiled, laughed, and cheered as Choppie twirled his propellers. The other flyers had never seen anything like it before. Choppie got a big smile and felt all happy inside.

It was then that all the flyers realized Choppie was fun and nice, and on the inside, he was just like them. Even though he looked different on the outside, the flyers and Choppie remained friends for years to come.

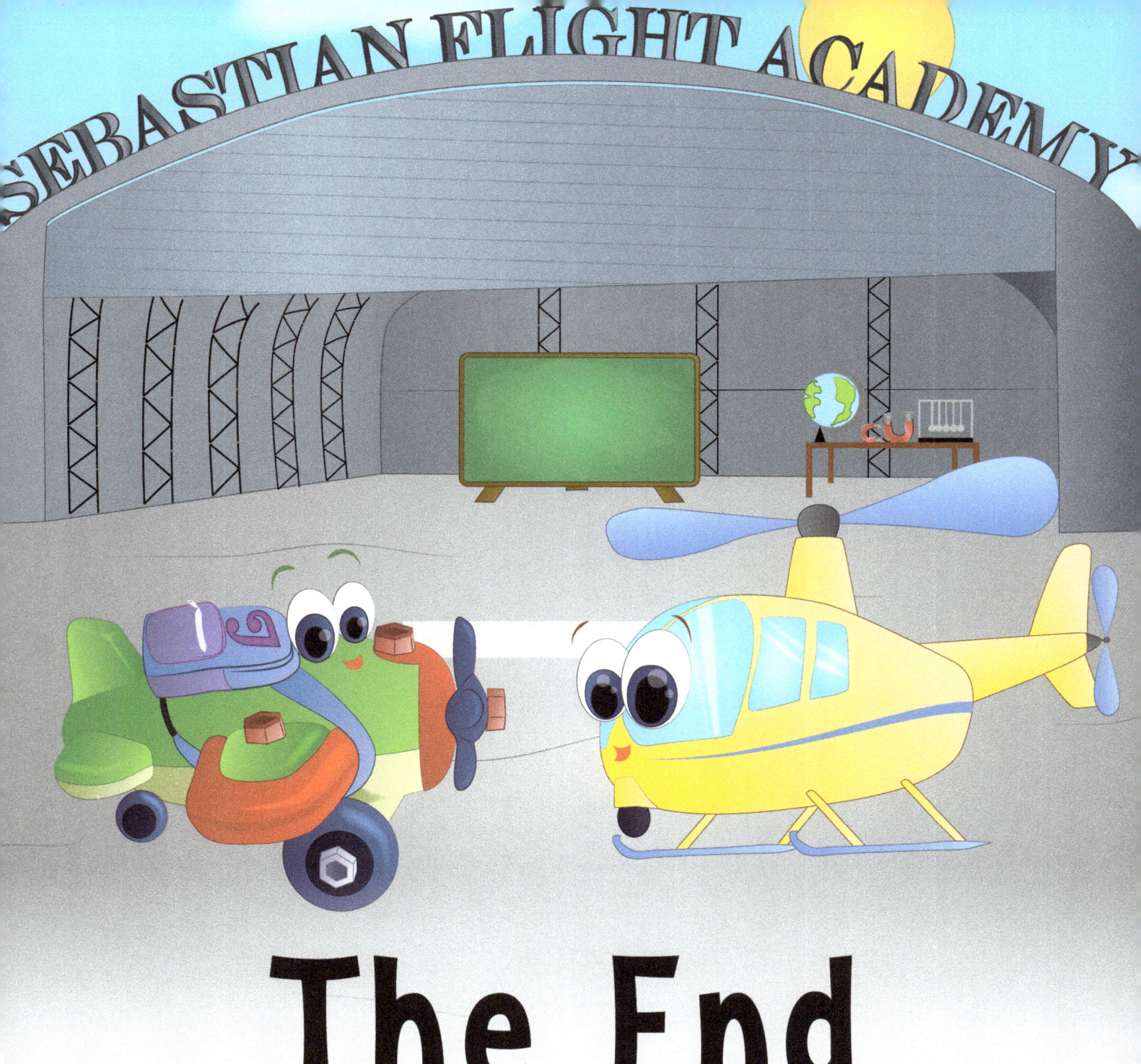